THE SECRETS OF HEALTHY RELATIONSHIPS

THE KEYS TO LASTING CONNECTIONS

DR. JAGADEESH PILLAI

Made with ♥ on the Notion Press Platform
www.notionpress.com

|| Dedicated to all wisdom seekers around the world ||

Contents

Contents

Prayer

"Om Bhadram Karnebhih Shrunuyaama DevaahBhadram Pashyemaakshabhiryajatraah SthirairangaistushtuvaamsastanoobhihVyashema Devahitam YadaayuhSwasti Na Indro VridhashravaahSwasti Nah Pooshaa VishwavedaahSwasti Nastaarkshyo ArishtanemihSwasti No Brihaspatir DadhaatuOm Shantih, Shantih, Shantih"

The literal meaning of this mantra is: OM. O Gods! Let us hear auspicious words from our ears. O reverent Gods! Let us behold propitious visions from our eyes, let our organs and body be stable, healthy, and strong. Let us do that which is pleasing to the gods in the life span allotted to us. May Indra, inscribed in the scriptures, bring us fortune! May Pushan, the knower of the world, grant us prosperity! May Trakshya, who vanquishes enemies, bestow us with blessings! May Brihaspati bring us success!
OM Peace, Peace, Peace.

About The Author

Dr. Jagadeesh Pillai is a renowned Guinness World Record holder, writer, and researcher hailing from Varanasi, also known as the abode of Lord Shiva. With a Ph.D. in Vedic Science and a range of creative ideas and achievements, he is a true polymath. He is the author of more than 100 books including Research Publications. Although his roots can be traced back to Kerala, the people of Varanasi hold him in high regard and affectionately consider him one of their own.

Dr. Pillai has achieved four Guinness World Records in the following subjects:

"Script to Screen" - In this record, Dr. Pillai produced and directed an animation film within the shortest time possible, breaking the previous record set by Canadians. He has also received numerous national and international awards and recognitions for this achievement.

Longest Line of Postcards - For this record, Dr. Pillai created a line of 16,300 postcards on the occasion of the 163rd anniversary of Indian Postal Day. The event also included a questionnaire about the Indian flag.

Largest Poster Awareness Campaign - Dr. Pillai designed an awareness campaign on the subject of "Beti Bachao - Beti Padhao" (Save the Girl Child - Educate the Girl Child) to achieve this record.

Largest Envelope - In tribute to the Indian Prime Minister's

"Make in India" initiative, Dr. Pillai created a 4000 square meter envelope using waste paper to achieve this record.

Attempted - **70000 Candles on a 210 kg Cake** - To celebrate the 70th Indian Independence Day, Dr. Pillai attempted to light 70,000 candles on a 210 kg cake, which was recorded in World Records India.

Attempted - **Documentary on Dhamek Stupa of Sarnath in 17 Languages** - Dr. Pillai attempted to create a documentary on the Dhamek Stupa of Sarnath, dubbing it in 17 different languages. The result of this attempt is currently awaiting confirmation from the Guinness World Records.

Dr. Pillai is skilled in teaching the Bhagavad Gita, a Hindu scripture, and is popular among young people. He has helped many young people improve their lives through his motivational teachings.

In addition to teaching, he has composed and sung numerous Sanskrit Bhajans and patriotic songs.

He has also written and directed several short films and documentaries for awareness campaigns, and has volunteered with the police in both UP and Kerala to spread awareness about various issues through videos and photography.

Incredibly, he has produced and directed over 100 documentaries about the city of Varanasi, all on his own.

He has also helped and guided more than 25 boys and girls to achieve world records through creative and innovative methods. He is a multifaceted person who uses his intellect and the blessings given to him by God to excel in various areas. He is both a teacher and a student, always learning and teaching, and is able to master any subject he comes across.

He is a selfless social activist and motivational speaker who has overcome struggles and failures to become a successful and enthusiastic individual with a rich life experience.

In addition to his work with the Bhagavad Gita, he is also an efficient Tarot card reader, Astro-Vastu consultant, and a talented singer and composer. He has sung the entire Ram Charita Manas and Bhagavad Gita in his own compositions, and has sung the phrase "Lokah Samastha Sukhino Bhavantu" in 50 different languages. He is currently working on a detailed and scientific study of Vedas, Upanishads, Puranas, and the Bhagavad Gita. He has also composed and sung the Hanuman Chalisa and Gayatri Mantra in 108 and 1008 different compositions, respectively.

Awards - Four Times Guinness World Records, Winner of Mahatma Gandhi Vishwa Shanti Puraskar, Mahatma Gandhi Global Peace Ambassador, Kashi Ratna Award, Dr. APJ Abdul Kalam Motivational Person of the Year 2017, Mother Teresa Award, Indira Gandhi Priyadarshini Award, Bharat Vikas Ratna Award, Udyog Ratna Award, Vigyan Prasar Award, Poorvanchal Ratn Samman.

PREFACE

In this book, "The Secrets of Healthy Relationships: The Keys to Lasting Connections", we explore the various aspects of what makes a relationship healthy and strong. We delve into the importance of communication, trust, intimacy, and the importance of working on oneself and one's relationship.

Throughout the book, we provide practical tips and strategies for building and maintaining a healthy relationship. We cover topics such as learning how to grow together as a couple, appreciating your differences, picking your battles, and building intimacy. Each chapter is designed to help you and your partner deepen your connection and strengthen your bond.

We understand that relationships can be challenging, and no two relationships are the same. However, by understanding the fundamental principles of what makes a relationship healthy, you can improve your relationship and make it a source of joy and fulfillment.

This book is not just for those who are in a romantic relationship, but for anyone looking to improve their connection with others. The principles discussed in this book can be applied to friendships, family relationships, and even professional relationships.

In this book, we hope to provide you with the tools and insights you need to create a strong, healthy, and lasting relationship. Whether you're just starting out or have been together for years, the secrets to a healthy relationship are within reach.

We invite you to read this book with an open mind and a willingness to learn and grow. We hope that you will find the information and strategies presented in this book to be helpful and that you will be able to apply them to your own relationship.

Let's embark on this journey together to discover the secrets of healthy relationships and to learn the keys to lasting connections.

I

Understanding Healthy Relationships - Exploring the characteristics of a healthy relationship

A healthy relationship is one in which both partners feel valued, respected, and supported. A healthy relationship is characterized by open communication, mutual trust, and a sense of shared responsibility. In a healthy relationship, both partners feel safe to express their thoughts, feelings, and needs without fear of judgment or rejection.

One of the most important characteristics of a healthy relationship is open and honest communication. This means that both partners feel comfortable expressing their thoughts, feelings, and needs and that they are willing to listen to and understand each other's perspectives. Open communication also means that both partners are able to express their concerns and work together to find solutions to problems.

Another key characteristic of a healthy relationship is mutual trust. Trust is built on honesty, reliability, and consistency. In a healthy relationship, both partners trust each other to keep their promises and to be there for each other when needed. Trust also means being able to rely on each other to be honest and to respect each other's boundaries.

Shared responsibility is also an important characteristic of a healthy relationship. This means that both partners take an active role in maintaining the relationship and that they are willing to work together to achieve their goals. Shared responsibility also means that both partners are willing to compromise and to make sacrifices for the sake of the relationship.

A healthy relationship is also characterized by mutual respect. This means that both partners are willing to listen to and understand each other's perspectives, and that they are willing to accept and respect each other's differences.

In addition to the above characteristics, a healthy

relationship also involves emotional and physical safety, mutual support, and a sense of shared values and goals. A healthy relationship is built on a foundation of mutual respect, trust, and open communication. It is important to note that healthy relationships require effort and commitment to maintain and grow.

Understanding the characteristics of a healthy relationship is important for building and maintaining a lasting connection. A healthy relationship is characterized by open communication, mutual trust, shared responsibility, mutual respect, emotional and physical safety, mutual support, and shared values and goals. It is important to be aware of these characteristics and to strive to incorporate them into your own relationships.

"A healthy relationship is built on trust, communication, and mutual growth."

II

Building a Foundation - Establishing trust and communication

Trust and communication are the foundation of any healthy relationship. Without trust and open communication, a relationship cannot thrive. Building a foundation of trust and communication takes time and effort, but it is essential for creating a lasting connection.

Establishing trust in a relationship means being open, honest, and reliable. It means keeping your promises and being there for your partner when they need you. Trust also means being willing to share your thoughts, feelings, and needs with your partner and being open to hearing theirs in return. Building trust takes time and effort, but it is essential for a healthy relationship.

Open and honest communication is also essential for building a strong foundation in a relationship. It means being willing to listen to and understand your partner's perspective and to express your own thoughts and feelings in a clear and respectful manner. Effective communication also requires active listening, empathy, and an understanding of non-verbal cues.

Both trust and communication are closely related and mutually dependent. Trust helps in effective communication and effective communication helps to build trust. For example, open and honest communication can help to build trust by increasing transparency and understanding between partners, whereas trust enables open communication by creating a safe space for both partners to express themselves honestly.

One way to establish trust and communication is to set clear boundaries and expectations from the start of the relationship. This means being clear about what you are comfortable with and what you are not, and being willing to communicate this to your partner. Setting boundaries also means being willing to listen to and respect your partner's boundaries.

Another way to establish trust and communication is to make an effort to understand and empathize with your partner's perspective. This means taking the time to listen and understand their thoughts and feelings and to show them that you care about their well-being.

Building a foundation of trust and communication is essential for creating a healthy and lasting relationship. It takes time and effort, but it is worth it in the long run. Clear communication and boundaries, effective listening, empathy, and understanding are some of the key ways to establish trust and communication in a relationship.

"In a healthy relationship, differences are celebrated and not suppressed."

☙

III

Listening and Feeling Heard - Learning to listen and be heard

In any relationship, it is essential to feel heard and understood. This is where active listening comes in. Active listening is a communication technique that involves paying attention, understanding, and responding to your partner's thoughts and feelings.

Active listening involves giving your full attention to your partner when they are speaking. This means putting away distractions, making eye contact, and truly listening to what they have to say. It also means asking clarifying questions and repeating back what you have heard to ensure that you understand their perspective.

Active listening also involves understanding and empathizing with your partner's thoughts and feelings. This means trying to see things from their point of view and showing that you care about their well-being. It also means being able to validate their emotions, even if you don't agree with them.

Feeling heard and understood is essential for building trust and communication in a relationship. When your partner feels that you are truly listening to them and understanding their perspective, they are more likely to open up and trust you with their thoughts and feelings.

Being heard and understood also means being able to express your own thoughts and feelings in a safe and respectful environment. In a healthy relationship, both partners should feel comfortable expressing themselves and should be heard and understood by the other.

It's important to note that, effective listening is a two-way street, it's not just about your partner listening to you but also about you listening to them. It's important to take turns and give each other an opportunity to speak and to be heard.

Learning to listen and be heard is essential for building a healthy and lasting relationship. Active listening, empathy, and understanding are key to making your partner feel heard and understood. Giving and taking turns in communication, and creating a safe and respectful environment for expressing thoughts and feelings are also important for building trust and communication in a relationship.

"Picking your battles wisely is key to maintaining a healthy and harmonious relationship."

ꝏ

IV

Demonstrating Loyalty and Respect - Understanding the importance of loyalty and respect

Loyalty and respect are two essential components of a healthy relationship. They are the foundation on which trust and communication are built. When both partners demonstrate loyalty and respect towards each other, the relationship is more likely to be strong, stable, and long-lasting.

Loyalty is the willingness to be there for your partner, to be supportive, and to stand by them through thick and thin. It means being honest, trustworthy, and dependable. Loyalty is about being committed to the relationship and being willing to put in the effort to make it work. It's about being willing to make sacrifices for your partner and being there for them when they need you.

Respect is the willingness to acknowledge and appreciate the value of your partner as an individual. It means treating your partner with dignity, honor, and esteem. Respect is about understanding and accepting your partner's thoughts, feelings, and needs, even if you don't always agree with them. It's about being willing to compromise and to work together to find solutions.

When both partners demonstrate loyalty and respect, the relationship is built on a foundation of trust and mutual understanding. Trust is built on loyalty, and respect is the foundation of trust. When a partner demonstrates loyalty, the other partner is more likely to trust them and open up to them. When a partner demonstrates respect, the other partner is more likely to feel valued and appreciated, and to trust them.

Loyalty and respect are also essential for building intimacy in a relationship. Intimacy is built on trust, and trust is built on loyalty and respect. When a partner feels that they can trust their partner and that their partner respects them, they are more likely to open up and to share their thoughts and feelings. This leads to deeper and more meaningful connections.

When one partner demonstrates loyalty and respect, the

other partner is more likely to reciprocate. This creates a positive feedback loop in the relationship, where both partners feel valued, respected, and appreciated.

Loyalty and respect are also important for maintaining a healthy relationship in difficult times. When a relationship is going through a tough time, loyalty and respect are the glue that holds it together. When both partners are loyal and respectful, they are more likely to work together to find solutions and to get through the difficult times.

Loyalty and respect are essential components of a healthy relationship. They are the foundation on which trust and communication are built. When both partners demonstrate loyalty and respect, the relationship is more likely to be strong, stable, and long-lasting. Loyalty and respect are essential for building trust, intimacy, and for maintaining a healthy relationship in difficult times. They are key to making a relationship work and to last.

"Intimacy is the glue that binds a healthy relationship together."

V

Setting Initial Expectations - Understanding the importance of setting expectations"

Expectations play a critical role in any relationship. They help to establish boundaries, create a sense of security, and provide a sense of direction for the relationship. Setting initial expectations is an important step in building a healthy and lasting relationship.

Expectations are the ideas and beliefs we have about how things should be in a relationship. They can be about anything from communication to finances, from sex to household responsibilities, and from emotional support to future plans. Expectations can be positive or negative, realistic or unrealistic, and they can change over time.

When expectations are not met, it can lead to disappointment, frustration, and even resentment. This is why it is important to set initial expectations early on in the relationship. When expectations are clearly defined, both partners understand what is expected of them and can work together to meet those expectations.

Setting expectations also helps to establish boundaries. Boundaries are the limits that we set in a relationship to protect ourselves and to ensure that we are treated with respect. Setting boundaries allows both partners to express their needs and to feel safe in the relationship.

When initial expectations are set, it also provides a sense of direction for the relationship. It gives both partners a clear understanding of where the relationship is headed and what they can expect from each other. This helps to create a sense of security and to build trust in the relationship.

It is important to note that, setting expectations does not mean that one partner should control the other or impose their own expectations on the other. Both partners should have a say in setting the expectations and be willing to work together to achieve them. It's important for both partners to be open to discussing and adjusting expectations as the relationship evolves.

Setting initial expectations is an important step in building a healthy and lasting relationship. Expectations help to establish boundaries, create a sense of security, and provide a sense of direction for the relationship. When initial expectations are set, it allows both partners to understand what is expected of them, to work together to meet those expectations and to build trust in the relationship. It's important for both partners to be open to discussing and adjusting expectations as the relationship evolves.

"Making time for each other is essential for building and maintaining a strong connection."

ꕥ

VI

Practicing Empathy - Developing empathy for your partner

Empathy is the ability to understand and share the feelings of another person. In a relationship, empathy is essential for building trust, understanding, and connection. It allows both partners to feel heard and understood, and to build a deeper understanding of each other's thoughts and feelings.

Empathy involves putting yourself in your partner's shoes and understanding their perspective. It means listening to their thoughts and feelings without judgment, and being able to validate and acknowledge their emotions, even if you don't agree with them. It also means being able to understand and relate to their experiences, even if they are different from your own.

Practicing empathy in a relationship helps to build trust and communication. When a partner feels that their thoughts and feelings are understood and validated, they are more likely to open up and trust their partner with their thoughts and feelings. This leads to better communication and a deeper understanding of each other.

Empathy also helps to build intimacy in a relationship. Intimacy is built on trust, and trust is built on understanding and connection. When a partner feels that their partner understands and relates to their thoughts and feelings, they are more likely to open up and share their thoughts and feelings. This leads to deeper and more meaningful connections.

Practicing empathy in a relationship also helps to resolve conflicts. When both partners are able to understand and relate to each other's perspectives, they are more likely to find common ground and to work together to find solutions. Empathy helps to create a sense of mutual understanding and respect, which is essential for resolving conflicts in a healthy way.

It's important to note that, practicing empathy does not mean that one partner should put their own feelings aside to prioritize the other's. It's important for both partners to practice empathy and to understand and validate each other's emotions. It's also important to remember that empathy is a skill that can be developed and improved over time.

Practicing empathy is essential for building trust, understanding, and connection in a relationship. It allows both partners to feel heard and understood and to build a deeper understanding of each other's thoughts and feelings. Practicing empathy helps to build trust, intimacy, and to resolve conflicts in a healthy way. It's important for both partners to practice empathy and to understand and validate each other's emotions, and it's a skill that can be developed and improved over time.

"Open and honest communication is the foundation of a healthy relationship."

ꕥ

VII

Communicating Effectively - Learning how to communicate effectively"

Effective communication is the key to any successful relationship. It allows both partners to express themselves, to understand each other's thoughts and feelings, and to work together to solve problems. Effective communication is a skill that can be learned and developed over time.

Effective communication involves being able to express yourself clearly and effectively. This means being able to use words and body language to convey your thoughts and feelings in a way that is easily understood by your partner.

It also means being able to listen actively, to understand and acknowledge your partner's perspective, and to respond in a way that shows that you care.

Effective communication also involves being able to resolve conflicts effectively. Conflict is an inevitable part of any relationship, and it's important to be able to work through conflicts in a healthy way. This means being able to express your thoughts and feelings in a way that is respectful and non-confrontational, and being able to listen to your partner's thoughts and feelings without judgment.

Effective communication also involves being able to communicate your needs and wants effectively. This means being able to express your needs and wants in a clear and direct way, and being able to negotiate with your partner to find solutions that work for both of you.

It is important to remember that effective communication is a two-way street. It's not just about expressing yourself effectively but also about being able to listen and understand your partner's perspective. It's important to take turns in communication and to give each other an opportunity to express their thoughts and feelings.

Effective communication is the key to any successful relationship. It allows both partners to express themselves, to understand each other's thoughts and feelings, and to work together to solve problems. Effective communication is a skill that can be learned and developed over time, it involves being able to express yourself clearly, to listen actively, and to resolve conflicts effectively, and to communicate your needs and wants in a clear and direct way. It's important to remember that effective communication is a two-way street and to take turns in communication and to give each other an opportunity to express their thoughts and feelings.

"Being on the same page about your relationship's goals and values is crucial for intimacy."

ᘓ

VIII

Growing Together - Learning how to grow together as a couple"

In any relationship, it is important for both individuals to constantly work on themselves and their connection with one another. Growing together as a couple means actively making an effort to improve yourselves and your relationship, rather than just letting things happen naturally.

One of the most important things to remember when growing together as a couple is that it is a two-way street. Both individuals need to be committed to working on the relationship and themselves, and they should be willing to make changes and compromise.

One way to grow together is to set shared goals. These can be personal goals, such as working on physical fitness or financial stability, or relationship goals, such as planning a vacation or improving communication. Setting shared goals gives both individuals a sense of purpose and direction, and working towards them together can bring you closer as a couple.

Another way to grow together is to make sure that you are constantly learning from one another. This means being open to feedback and being willing to listen to one another's perspectives and experiences. It also means taking the time to understand and appreciate one another's strengths and weaknesses, and learning how to work with them.

Learning how to communicate effectively is also essential for growing together as a couple. This means being able to express your thoughts, feelings, and needs in a way that is clear and respectful, and it also means being able to listen actively to your partner.

It's also important to make sure that you are both on the same page when it comes to your relationship. This means discussing important issues, such as your shared values and goals, and making sure that you both have a similar vision for the future.

Finally, make time for each other. It's easy to get caught up in the day-to-day grind and neglect your relationship, but taking the time to be present and fully engaged with each other is crucial for growing together. This can be as simple as having dinner together or taking a walk, but it's important to make sure that you are spending quality time together.

Growing together as a couple is about actively making an effort to improve yourselves and your relationship. It's about setting shared goals, learning from one another, communicating effectively, being on the same page, and making time for each other. With the right mindset and effort, any couple can grow stronger and deeper in love.

"Creating shared goals and working towards them together can bring you closer as a couple."

ꕤ

IX

Appreciating Your Differences - Understanding the importance of appreciating differences

In any relationship, it is essential to understand and appreciate the differences between you and your partner. These differences can include things like personality, values, and interests, and they play a significant role in shaping who you both are as individuals.

One of the most important things to remember when it comes to appreciating differences is that they are what make us unique. Instead of trying to change or suppress these differences, it is important to embrace and celebrate them. This means being open to new experiences and perspectives, and being willing to learn from one another.

Appreciating differences also means being able to communicate effectively about them. This means being able to express your thoughts, feelings, and needs in a way that is clear and respectful, and it also means being able to listen actively to your partner. When you can communicate openly and honestly about your differences, you can find common ground and work through any conflicts that may arise.

Another important aspect of appreciating differences is being able to compromise. This means being willing to make sacrifices and adjustments to accommodate your partner's needs and preferences. It also means being willing to negotiate and find solutions that work for both of you.

It's also important to make sure that you are both on the same page when it comes to your relationship. This means discussing important issues, such as your shared values and goals, and making sure that you both have a similar vision for the future.

Finally, make time for each other. It's easy to get caught up in the day-to-day grind and neglect your relationship, but taking the time to be present and fully engaged with each other is crucial for growing together. This can be as simple as having dinner together or taking a walk, but it's important to make sure that you are spending quality time together.

Appreciating differences is essential for any relationship. It's about embracing and celebrating the unique qualities that make you and your partner who you are, communicating effectively, being able to compromise, being on the same page, and making time for each other. With the right mindset and effort, any couple can learn to appreciate and respect each other's differences, and grow stronger in their relationship.

"Vulnerability and honesty are the path to intimacy and deeper connection."

X

Picking Your Battles - Learning how to pick your battles

In any relationship, it is important to learn how to pick your battles. This means being able to discern which issues are worth fighting for and which are not. This can be a difficult skill to master, but it is essential for maintaining a healthy and harmonious relationship.

One of the most important things to remember when it comes to picking your battles is that not every disagreement or conflict is worth fighting over. Some issues may not be worth the energy and effort, while others may be more important and require a more assertive response.

One way to pick your battles is to focus on the bigger

picture. This means taking a step back and looking at the overall situation and how it might affect your relationship in the long term. If the issue at hand is not likely to have a significant impact on the overall health of your relationship, it may not be worth fighting over.

Another way to pick your battles is to focus on what is important to you and your partner. This means being able to identify the underlying needs and values that are driving your conflict and being willing to compromise and find a solution that meets the needs of both parties.

It's also important to learn how to communicate effectively. This means being able to express your thoughts, feelings, and needs in a way that is clear and respectful, and it also means being able to listen actively to your partner. When you can communicate openly and honestly, you can find common ground and work through any conflicts that may arise

Finally, make time for each other. It's easy to get caught up in the day-to-day grind and neglect your relationship, but taking the time to be present and fully engaged with each other is crucial for growing together. This can be as simple as having dinner together or taking a walk, but it's important to make sure that you are spending quality time together.

Picking your battles is an essential skill for any relationship. It's about being able to discern which issues are worth fighting for, focusing on the bigger picture, identifying underlying needs and values, communicating effectively, and making time for each other. With the right mindset and effort, any couple can learn to pick their battles and maintain a healthy and harmonious relationship.

"A healthy relationship is a journey of constant learning, growth and evolution."

ཙ

XI

Building Intimacy - Developing strategies for building intimacy

Intimacy is an essential part of any healthy relationship. It is the emotional and physical closeness that allows couples to connect on a deeper level and strengthen their bond. Building intimacy requires time, effort, and commitment from both individuals, but with the right strategies, it can be achieved.

One of the most important things to remember when building intimacy is to make time for each other. This means setting aside time each day or week to be alone with your partner and focus on building your connection. It can be as simple as having dinner together, taking a walk, or just sitting and talking. The key is to make sure that you are spending quality time together.

Another strategy for building intimacy is to communicate effectively. This means being able to express your thoughts, feelings, and needs in a way that is clear and respectful, and it also means being able to listen actively to your partner. When you can communicate openly and honestly, you can understand each other better and build trust and intimacy.

It's also important to be open and vulnerable with your partner. This means being willing to share your thoughts, feelings, and experiences, and being willing to listen and understand your partner's as well. This can be difficult, but it is essential for building intimacy.

Another strategy is to make physical touch a priority. This means taking the time to hug, kiss, and hold each other, and make sure that physical touch is a regular part of your relationship. This can help to build emotional intimacy and help you feel more connected to your partner.

Finally, make sure that you are both on the same page when it comes to your relationship. This means discussing important issues, such as your shared values and goals, and making sure that you both have a similar vision for the future. This can help to build intimacy by ensuring that you are both working towards the same goals and have a shared sense of purpose.

Building intimacy is an essential part of any healthy relationship. It requires time, effort, and commitment from both individuals. Strategies for building intimacy include making time for each other, communicating effectively, being open and vulnerable, making physical touch a priority, and being on the same page about your relationship. With the right mindset and effort, any couple can build intimacy and strengthen their bond.

OTHER BOOKS OF THE AUTHOR

1. The Moments When I Met God
2. Kashiyile Theertha Pathangal
3. GURU GYAN VANI
4. Abhiprerak Gita
5. ASSI SE JAIN GHAT TAK
6. Hopelessness of Arjuna
7. The Soul and It's True Nature
8. Sense of Action (Karma)
9. Action through Wisdom
10. Action through Wisdom
11. THEORY AND PRACTICAL OF EVERY ACTION
12. LOGICAL UNDERSTANDING OF THE SUPREME
13. THE IMPERISHABLE SUPREME
14. Yatra Nishadraj se Hanuman Ghat Tak
15. Yatra Karnatak Ghat se Raja Ghat Tak
16. Yatra Pandey Ghat se Prayagraj Ghat Tak
17. Yatra Ranjendra Prasad Ghat se Dattatreya Ghat Tak
18. YaatraSindhiya Ghat se Gwaliar Ghat Tak
19. Yatra Mangala Gauri Ghat se Hanuman Gadhi Ghat Tak
20. Yatra Gaay Ghat Se Nishad Ghat Tak
21. MAA GANGA, GHATEN EVM UTSAV
22. Ganga Arti Dev Deepavali evam Any Utsav
23. Potentials of Digitalized India
24. VEDIC CONSCIOUSNESS
25. A Brief Introduction to Vedic Science
26. Kashi ke Barah Jyotirling
27. IMPACT OF MOTIVATION
28. Let's have a Milky Way Journey
29. Color Therapy in a Nutshell

30. Rigveda in a Nutshell
31. Yajurveda in a Nutshell
32. Samveda in a Nutshell
33. Atharva Veda in a Nutshell
34. Ayushman Bhava - Ayurveda
35. Srimad Bhagavad Gita and Upanishad Connection
36. Srimad Bhagavad Gita - an attempt to summarize each chapter.
37. Facts and Impact of Nakshatra
38. Astro Gems - NAVARATNA
39. Ekadashi - A Concise Overview
40. A Concise View of Hanuman Chalisa
41. Inspirational Gita
42. Nakshatraranyam
43. Summary of 18 Mahapuranas
44. Synopsis of 18 Upa Puranas
45. Rigvediya Upanishads
46. Shukla Yajurvediya Upanishads
47. Krishna Yajurvediya Upanishads
48. Samavediya Upanishads
49. Atharvavediya Upanishads
50. The Seven Great Sages
51. From Rocket Scientist to President Dr. APJ Abdul Kalam
52. The Visionary's Voice - Quotes of Dr. APJ Abdul Kalam
53. The Wisdom of Swami Vivekananda: Insights and Inspiration from a Legendary Spiritual Teacher
54. Ayurvedic Remedies from the Garden
55. Sages and Seers
56. Rising Strong – Motivational Stories of Women
57. Beyond Flames -Mystery stories of Funeral Ghat Manikarnika
58. The Origins of Tulsi: A Look at the Mythological Roots of the Plant"

59. The Holistic Cow: A Look at the Physical, Spiritual, and Cultural Importance of Cows in India
60. Arts of Healing
61. Exploring the Divine
62. Understanding Five Elements
63. The Etymology of Ram
64. Symbols of India
65. Voice of Change (About Speeches of Great Men)
66. She Speaks (About Speeches of Great Women)
67. Patriotism on Celluloid – Brief About Patriotic Films
68. The Music of Motivation: A Brief Guide to Inspirational Film Songs
69. **Unlocking the Secrets of the Dashopanishads**
70. A Cultural Mosaic
71. Ancient Traditions, Modern Minds
72. Ecos of Ancient Wisdom
73. Beneath the Surface
74. From Temples to Ashrams
75. Sages of the Subcontinent
76. The Art of Healling (Ayurveda, Yoga & Naturopathy)
77. Indian Kitchen
78. The Festivals of India
79. The Indian Epics Retold
80. The Power of Mantras
81. The Indian River Ganges
82. The Indian Architecture
83. Rites of Passage
84. The Indian Silk Road
85. The Indian Literature
86. The Indian Villages
87. The Indian Folks & Crafts
88. The Way of Buddha
89. The Ramayan of Tulsidas

90. Astrological Remedies
91. The Secret Power of Motivation
92. Secret of Developing your Inner Strength
93. The Secret Path to Motivation
94. The Art and Secret of Positive Thinking
95. The Secrets of Practicing Ethical Living
96. Indian Art and Painting
97. The Indian Herbalism
98. Bharatanatyam to Kathak
99. Exploring India's Astrological Remedies
100. The Indian Festival of Flowers
101. Indian Handicrafts
102. The Splashes of Joy – India's Colour Festival

CONTACT

DR. JAGADEESH PILLAI

PhD in Vedic Science

Four Times Guinness World Record Holder

Winner of Mahatma Gandhi Vishwa Shanti Puraskar and Global Peace Ambassador

Gemology, Astro & Vastu Consultant - Spiritual Counselor

Consultant for designing World Record Ideas

Efficient Tarot Card Reader

9839093003

myrichindia@gmail.com

drjagadeeshpillai@facebook

drjagadeeshpillai@instagram

jagadeeshpillai@youtube

www. JAGADEESHPILLAI.com

|| LOKAHA SAMASTHAHA SUKHINO BHAVANTU ||

9 798889 517597

Printed by Libri Plureos GmbH in Hamburg, Germany